National Sailing Scheme Syllabus & Logbook

国家航海计划教学大纲及日志

英国皇家游艇协会 **著**
顾 禹 **译**

The Royal Yachting Association, RYA House, Ensign Way, Hamble,
Southampton, Hampshire SO31 4YA
www.rya.org.uk

哈爾濱工程大學出版社
Harbin Engineering University Press

INTRODUCTION 简介

航海是一项奇妙而多样化的运动，适合所有人参与。在这部《国家航海计划教学大纲及日志》中教学计划设计的目的是帮助你去享受这项吸引人的运动。该书中的所有课程都可以在小帆船、龙骨船或多体帆船上进行讲授，所以你能够在任何你所希望的船型上学习这门课程。

Amanda Van Santen
阿曼达·范·萨腾
RYA Chief Instructor, Dinghy & Windsurfing
英国皇家游艇协会总教练，小帆船和帆板

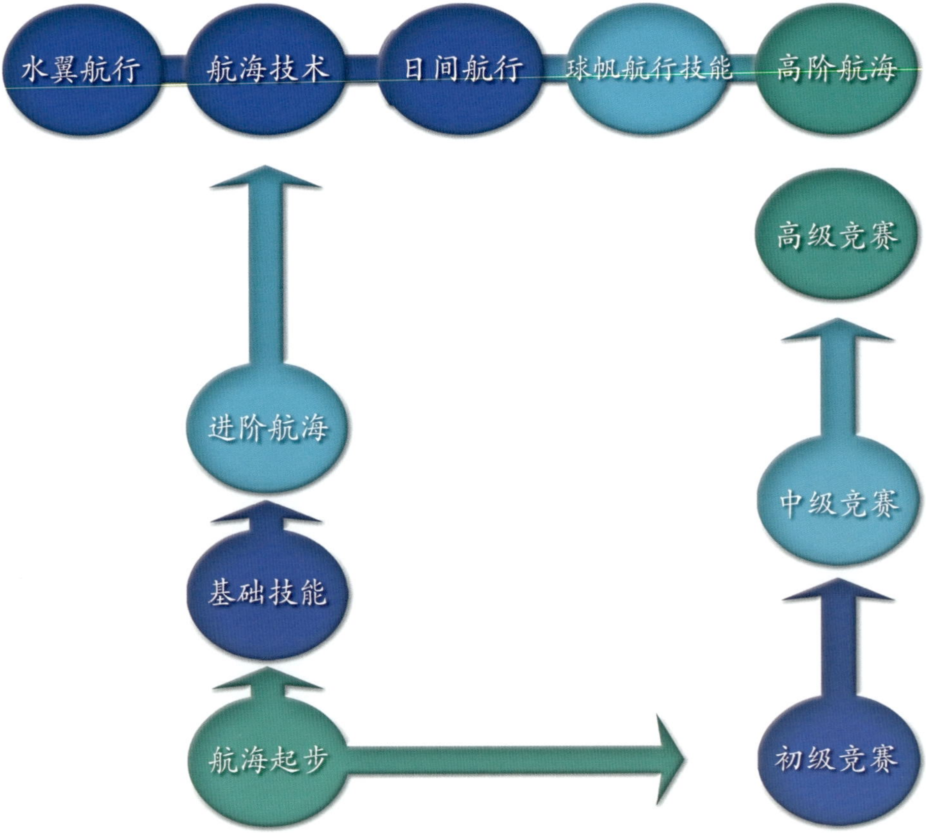

目录 CONTENTS

CONTENTS 目录

How to find the right sailing course? 如何找到适合的帆船课程？

The reputation of the RYA National Sailing Scheme has been built on high standards and good tuition. RYA Training Centres vary according to the sailing area available and the type of boats and level of tuition on offer. Whether you wish to learn to sail locally or improve your sailing on holiday, there should be an RYA Training Centre to suit you. To select a course that will meet your needs, visit the RYA website www.rya.org.uk/wheresmynearest for a list of sailing schools near you.

英国皇家游艇协会（简称 RYA）航海计划的声誉是建立在高标准和优秀的教学基础之上的。英国皇家游艇协会的培训中心是根据其可使用的航行区域、船只种类和可提供的教学水平来划分的。无论是在您附近的海域学习航海或者在假日期间提升您的航海技术，您都可以找到适合您的RYA培训中心。如要选择一个您所需要的课程，请登录RYA官方网站www.rya.org.uk/wheresmynearest选择您附近的航海学校。

Some RYA Training Centres have specialised facilities (including boats) for people with disabilities. Others can offer integrated courses in standard boats. Some students with disabilities may need additional help to complete the full requirements for an RYA certificate. There is provision within the Scheme for certificates to be endorsed as appropriate. Please contact the Principal of your selected RYA Training Centre or the RYA for more information.

部分RYA培训中心有为残疾人特别提供的设施（包括船只）。有些能够在标准船型上提供完整的课程。一些身体有残疾的学生可能需要额外的帮助来完成RYA认证课程。在我们的教学体系中有严格的规定来确保颁发合适的证书。请联系您所选择的RYA培训机构的负责人或者直接联系RYA来获取更多信息。

What is an RYA Recognised Training Centre? RYA认可的培训机构是什么样的？

Safety is a priority for the RYA. Each RYA Training Centre is regularly inspected for standards of tuition, facilities and equipment, as laid down by RYA Training and published in the guidance notes.All must have qualified staff, suitable boats and adequate safety cover. RYA Training Centres should display a Certificate of Recognition specifying the activities for which they are recognised. They are also required to carry public liability insurance.

安全是RYA第一考虑的。RYA对每一家培训中心都会定期地审查其教学水平、设施及设备，这在RYA的培训中有相关规定并印刷在培训指南中。每家培训中心都要求设有合格的培训人员、适合的船只和适当的安全保护措施。RYA培训中心应当展示一张认可证书标明这些机构被认可的活动项目。这些机构必需购买公共责任险。

For Beginners' courses run in single-handed dinghies, there should be an instructor to a maximum of 6 students in single-handed dinghies, or 1 to 3 in crewed dinghies with the instructor on board. Keelboat courses can be run with an instructor/student ratio of up to 1 to 4.

对于在单人小帆船上的初学课程，每位教练应最多配6个学员驾驶单人帆船。双人艇教学并且有教练陪同在船上的教练与学员比例最多是1:3。龙骨船课程教练与学员的比例最多可以为1:4。

Training carried out in coastal conditions that are not tidal should include the tidal material in the relevant sections.

即使在没有潮汐流的沿海水域进行训练，也应在相关部分包含关于潮汐的知识。

At the end of your course, the Principal or Chief Instructor will decide whether certificates

are to be awarded. Certificates are specific to the type of boat used, i.e. dinghy, keelboat or multihull. If the Principal decides that further practice is necessary before awarding you a certificate, they will explain the reasons to you. Should you feel it necessary to appeal against the outcome, contact RYA Training for guidance.
在课程的最后，是否颁发证书应由该机构负责人或总教练来决定。证书上应标明所使用的船型，如小帆船、龙骨船或者多体帆船。如果机构负责人决定在颁发证书前您还需要进行更多的练习，他们会向您说明原因。如果您想对结果进行上诉，请联系RYA培训中心。

The courses 课程

All the courses in the RYA National Sailing Scheme can be completed in just two days, or spread over a series of sessions covering a period of 16 hours. Most are flexible and often available as evening or half-day sessions.
RYA国家航海计划中的全部课程可以在两天内完成，也可拆分为一共用时16个小时的多节小课程。这些课程大多数是灵活的，而且可以提供晚间或半天课程。

Direct assessments 直接考核

Experienced sailors may wish to have direct assessment of their skills rather than taking part in a training course. The criteria are outlined in this book. Individual items will be signed off by the assessing instructor and the declaration signed by the Principal or Chief Instructor.
经验丰富的水手可能希望直接评估自己的技能，而不去参加培训课程。这本书中列出了相关标准。每项标准都要经过考核教练审批，并最终由机构负责人或总教练签署认可。

What next? 下一步是什么？

After taking your course you may consider joining a club, or buying a boat and joining the class association, who organise a variety of events. The RYA website (www.rya.org.uk) is a good place to find a club or locate your class association.
在完成课程之后，你可以考虑加入一家俱乐部，或购买自己的帆船并加入特定船型的协会组织，这些协会会举办多种活动。RYA官网(www.rya.org.uk)是一个搜索俱乐部和找到您船只级别协会的好地方。

How to become an instructor? 如何成为一名教练？

Having learnt to sail, you may enjoy passing your skills on to others. The RYA Instructor is an experienced sailor who has successfully completed a sailing test (the pre-entry test) and an instructor training course. Further information is on the RYA website.
学会了航海，你可能会乐于传授你的技能给其他人。一名RYA教练员也是一个经验丰富的水手，他/她已经成功地完成了航行测试（课前测试）和教练员培训课程。进一步的信息在RYA官网上可以找到。
RYA Instructors should also hold a first aid certificate and the RYA Powerboat Level 2 Certificate. Full details are contained in RYA publication G14, *RYA National Sailing Scheme Instructor Handbook*.
RYA教练员应持有急救证书和RYA机动艇2级证书。所有的细节都包含在RYA出版的G14：《国家航海计划教练手册》里面。

Courses for young people 青少年课程

The RYA also offers a training scheme for young people, the Youth Sailing Scheme. Full details are published in RYA book G11. Following completion of the Youth Sailing Scheme, young people may participate in further training through the advanced modules of the National Sailing Scheme.
RYA也提供了针对年轻人的培训方案，即青少年航海计划。该计划详情记录在

RYA G11的书里面。在完成青少年航海计划之后，青年人可通过国家航海计划的高级单元进行高级别的培训。

Windsurfing, Powerboating, Sail and Power Cruising 帆板、机动艇、帆和机动艇巡航

The RYA organises similar training schemes for all these activities. Full details are available from the website or the RYA Training Department.

RYA为这些活动组织类似的培训计划。详请可以在官网或RYA培训中心找到。

Learning resources 学习资源

The RYA produces a wide range of materials to help you learn, from course handbooks to training DVDs. These can be obtained through RYA Training Centres and the RYA website.

RYA出版了范围广泛的资料来帮助您学习，从课程手册到培训DVD。这些内容可以通过RYA培训中心和RYA官网获得。

THE DUKE OF EDINBURGH'S AWARD

> Are you aged between 14 to 24 and fancy challenging yourself?

The RYA is recognised as a National Operating Authority for The Duke of Edinburgh's Award (DofE). The DofE is a voluntary, non-competitive programme of activities for anyone aged 14 to 24, providing a fantastic opportunity to experience new activities or develop existing skills.

There are three progressive levels of programmes that, when successfully completed, lead to a Bronze, Silver or Gold Award.

Sailing as part of your DofE

Achieving a DofE Award can be made an adventure from beginning to end. Within an RYA club or training centre there are already many activities you could take part in that can count towards your DofE. These could range from:

Volunteering

Helping out at your local training centre, club or Team15 night on a regular basis. This could be as an assistant, in the kitchen or maybe even on the committee!

Physical

Regularly taking part in sailing or windsurfing activity? Why not set yourself a goal to gain a certain certificate in the RYA National Sailing or Windsurfing scheme, or maybe participate in regular club racing?

Skill

All about developing your skills, whether practical, social or personal. You may choose to sharpen up your powerboating, learn a new skill such as boat repair work, become an instructor or perhaps increase your theory knowledge and learn all about meteorology!

Residential and Expedition

You may never have been away from home before, let alone used your board or boat to go on an exciting adventure with friends, so now is the time!

Further information can be found, explaining the opportunities available, on the DofE website www.dofe.org, and the RYA website www.rya.org.uk/go/dofe.

爱丁堡公爵奖励计划

你是14到24岁梦想着挑战自己的年轻人吗?

RYA是公认的爱丁堡公爵奖励(简称DofE)国家权威运营机构。DofE是为1 4到2 4岁的青年人提供的一项自愿的、非竞争性的活动计划,旨在为青年人提供体验新活动或提高现有技能的极好的机会。

该计划设有三个晋升级别课程,当顺利完成之后,可获得青铜、白银或黄金奖项。

航海能否成为你DofE活动的一部分?

取得爱丁堡公爵奖可以说是一次彻头彻尾的探险过程。你可以在RYA俱乐部或培训中心里面参加很多活动来取得DofE的积分。其内容包括:

志愿者

长期在当地培训中心、俱乐部或Team15之夜(青少年帆板运动常规比赛)帮忙,这包括做一名助理、在厨房帮忙或者有可能进入委员会里面。

体能

你是否经常参与帆船或帆板运动?为什么不给自己制定一个目标去取得国家航海计划或帆板计划中的某个证书,或参与俱乐部举行的常规比赛呢?

技能

包括提升各种实用的、社交的或个人技能。你可以选择提高安全艇驾驶技术,学习一项新的技能,比如船只修理工作,成为一名教练员或丰富你的理论和气象学知识。

个人生活能力和探险

你可能从没有离开家生活过,更不用说使用你的帆板或帆船去和朋友进行一次很刺激的探险,现在你的机会来了!

更多关于相关信息的说明可以在DofE的官网www.dofe.org,和RYA的官网 www.rya.org.uk/go/dofe 上找到。

Level 1 – Start Sailing
级别一 航海起步

This course provides a short introduction to sailing for novices. By the end of the course you will have the basic understanding of dinghy-handling techniques and background knowledge. It is recommended that all participants consolidate this short introduction with the Basic Skills and Better Sailing courses.
这门课程是为初学航海者提供的简短的入门训练。在该课程结束之后，你将能够对小帆船操控技巧和理论知识有个基本的了解。我们建议所有学员把这门简介课程与“基础技能”和“进阶航海”这两门课程结合起来学习。

Duration: Approximately 16 hours (either spread over a series of sessions or 2 full days).
时长：大约16个小时（可以分为几节小课或两个整天课）。

> Practical 实操技能

Has a practical understanding of
在实践中掌握如下技能：

Rigging 装帆

Basic rigging, parts of the sail, sail controls and foils
基本索具，帆的组成部分，帆的控制器和片状部件

Has wind awareness ashore
能够在岸上感知的风

Sailing techniques and manoeuvres 航行技术及操控

Wind awareness afloat 在水上的风感

Reaching—sailing across the wind
横风行驶：穿越风航行

Stopping—Lying-to 停船：迎风停船

Controlling speed 控制船速

Getting out of irons 摆脱顶风停船

Tacking—turning the front of the boat through the wind 迎风转向：船头穿越风

Sailing upwind 迎风航行

The Five Essentials 航行五要素

Sailing downwind 顺风航行

Gybing—turning the back of the boat through the wind, from a training run
顺风转向：顺风航行时船尾穿越风

Importance of good communication when manoeuvring (double handers)
双人航行时保持良好的沟通的重要性

Can perform a basic capsize recovery, understands the importance of staying with the boat *(Optional)
能够完成一次基本的翻覆回正，知道人船不分的重要性*（可选项）

Launching and recovery* 下水及回岸

Can 能够：

Secure a boat on the trolley
把船只妥善安放在手推车里面

Understands the principles of 了解如下原则：

Wheeling a trolley clear of other boats and overhead cables
移动手推车时避免碰撞其他船只和上方线缆

Launching and leaving the shore
推船下水和离岸

Coming ashore and recovery of a boat
回岸和收船上岸

Ropework 结绳技巧

Can tie a figure of eight knot, round turn and two half hitches and secure a rope to a cleat
可以系一个8字结、木结和系羊角索

> Sailing Theory 航行理论

Has theoretical understanding of
掌握并理解如下知识：

Clothing and equipment 着装及装备

Knows the importance of personal safety, clothing and buoyancy

Level 1 – Start Sailing
级别一 航海起步

知道自身安全、着装和助浮衣的重要性

Sailing background 航海理论知识

An awareness of other water users
观察在同一水域航行的其他活动者

Basic rules of the road—Avoid a collision at all costs, power/sail, port/starboard, overtaking boat, windward boat
基础的航行规则：不惜一切代价避免碰撞，动力船让帆船，左舷船让右舷船，超越船让，上风船让下风船

Visual methods of attracting attention
引起其他船只视觉注意的方法

Meteorology 气象学

Has an awareness of onshore and offshore winds
认识向岸风和离岸风

Sources of weather information and their relevance
天气信息的来源和它们的用处：

Effects on sailing location
航行区域的影响

Beaufort Scale 蒲福风级

Conditions appropriate to ability and sailing location
选择与自身能力匹配的条件以及航行地点

> Keelboat Sailors 龙骨船水手

Clothing and equipment 着装和设备

Understands 理解：

Use of, and correct fitting of lifejackets
使用及调节救生衣

Use of a safety harness if fitted
知道如何使用安全带（如配备）

Man overboard recovery 救助落水人员

Understands 理解：

Actions to be taken to recover a man overboard
救助落水人员上船的步骤

Use of mooring lines 如何使用系泊绳

Emergency equipment and precautions
急救设备和注意事项

Has knowledge and awareness of
有如下物品的知识和常识：

Potential hazards of fuel and gas
燃气和燃料的潜在危险

Stowage and use of fire extinguishers
装载和使用灭火器

Other aspects 其他事项

Basic Skills Course 基本技能课程

> Chief Instructor's/Principal's Signature
总教练/校长签字

> RYA Training Centre
RYA 培训中心

*Not necessarily applicable to keelboats. 不适用于龙骨船

Level 2 – Basic Skills
级别二 基础技能

On completion of this course, you will have a basic knowledge of sailing and be capable of sailing without an instructor on board in light winds. It will be assumed that every student starting this course has already mastered the practical skills and absorbed the background knowledge required for Start Sailing. Both courses can be combined. Dinghy or multihull capsize recovery will be conducted in a controlled manner, one boat at a time, with a suitable rescue boat in attendance.
在完成这门课程后，你将会掌握基本的航行知识并有能力在小风天且在无教练陪同的情况下独立航行。我们要求开始学习这门课程的每一个学员都掌握了“航海起步”中的实践操作技能和理论知识。这两门课程可以放在一起学习。单体帆船和多体帆船的翻覆回正练习应该在可控的方式下进行，一次练习一只并配有安全艇在场。

Duration: Approximately 16 hours (either spread over a series of sessions or 2 full days).
时长：大约16个小时（可分为几节小课或两个整天的课程）

› Practical 实践操作

Has a practical understanding of
在实践中理解如下操作：

Rigging 装船

How to rig according to weather conditions
如何根据不同的天气情况装船 ■

Reefing ashore* 在岸上缩帆* ■

Sailing techniques and manoeuvres 航行技巧与操作

Leaving and returning to a beach, jetty or mooring
驶离和返回沙滩、码头或系泊处 ■

Coming alongside a moored boat
靠向已锚泊的船只 ■

Sailing in close company
与其他船只近距离组队航行 ■

Performing a man overboard recovery
完成一次落水人员救助 ■

Is aware of lee shore dangers
知道背风岸的危险 ■

The Five Essentials 航行五要素 ■

Can tack while sailing upwind, showing refined skill, losing minimal ground
可以在逆风航行时转向，展现高超的技术水平，并使用最佳迎风角度 ■

Can gybe in a controlled manner while sailing downwind
可以在顺风航行时平稳地顺风转向 ■

Shows good communication when manoeuvring (Double–handers)
驾驶双人船时表现出良好的沟通协调能力 ■

Understands and shows awareness of other water users
了解海域中其他活动者的动向 ■

Can sail around a short course using all points of sail and crewing skills
可以在短航线内使用全部角度航行以及作为缭手的技能 ■

Ropework 结绳术

Can tie a bowline, clove hitch and reef knot
能够系一个单套结、双套结和缩帆结 ■

Capsize recovery 翻覆回正

Can right a capsized boat using one method of righting and has knowledge of at least one other
能够使用一种方法回正一只翻了的船，并至少知道额外一种方法 ■

Racing 比赛

Understands the course and starting procedure (May be covered as onshore teaching)
了解竞赛航线及起航步骤（可以涵盖在岸上教学内） ■

Level 2 – Basic Skills 级别二 基础技能

Keelboat Sailors 龙骨船水手

Rigging 装船

Can reef afloat 能够在水上缩帆

Ropework 结绳术

Can use winches 能够使用绞盘

Use of engines (if fitted) 使用引擎（如果有安装）

Has knowledge of engine checks, starting, stopping and running procedures
知道检查引擎、启动、停止和驾驶的步骤

Can come alongside and pick up a mooring
能够停靠在系泊浮标旁并能拾起浮标

Sailing techniques and manoeuvres 航行技能及操控

Can 能够：

Anchor 锚泊

Sail using transits 使用参照线航行

Emergency equipment and precautions 急救设备及预防

Knows the importance of first aid kits and flares including stowage
了解急救箱和信号弹的重要性及存储方式

Multihull Sailors 多体船水手

Sailing techniques and manoeuvres 航行技巧与操控

Understands the basic principles of crew weight, airflow, technique (CAT)
了解关于船员体重、气流、技巧（简称CAT）的基本知识

Sailing Theory 航行理论

Has theoretical understanding of 理解如下知识：

Clothing and equipment 着装与设备

Knows the importance of personal safety, clothing, basic personal and boat buoyancy
知道安全设备、着装和基本的个人及船载助浮衣的重要性

Launching and recovery 下水及回岸

Boat storage ashore, launching and recovery
在岸上存放船只、下水及回岸

Sailing background 航海理论知识

Has knowledge of 有如下知识：

Basic rules of the road; avoid collisions at all costs, power/sail, port/starboard, windward boat, overtaking boat
基础的航行规则；不惜任何代价避免碰撞，动力船让帆船，左舷船让右舷船，上风船让下风船，让超越船

Basic advice for independent sailing 关于独立航行的基本建议：

Self-reliance and basic equipment
依靠自己和基础设备

Visual methods of attracting attention
引起视觉注意的方法

Has knowledge of 有如下知识：

The points of sailing and the 'No go Zone'
航行角度和“不可航行区域”

How a sail works 帆的原理

How a sailing boat moves (basic theory)
帆是如何推动船的（基本理论）

Meteorology 气象学

Has knowledge of 有如下知识：

Sources of relevant weather, inshore forecasts and their interpretation
相关天气信息的来源、近海的天气预报与解读

The Beaufort Wind Scale 蒲福风级

Understands when to reef 懂得何时缩帆

Has knowledge of a simple synoptic chart
了解简单的天气图

Level 2 – Basic Skills
级别二　基础技能

Understands 了解：

How to apply weather forecasts in coastal waters
如何在沿海水域利用天气预报

Tide tables, tidal sequence of springs and neaps, ebb and flow
潮汐表、大潮和小潮的前后过程，以及潮起和潮落

Speed over ground with/against tidal flow
顶流和顺流时的航速

The effect of wind direction and tidal flow on sailing conditions
风向和潮汐流对于航行的影响

The importance of informing someone ashore and the dangers of sailing alone
将你将出海的信息通知岸上人员的重要性和单独航行时可能出现的危险情况

Knows how to access local information and advice for sea sailing
知道如何获取当地海域信息和航行建议

Other aspects 其他事项

Better Sailing Course
进阶航海课程

Opportunities for regular activity (local club and centre activity and groups, etc.)
定期活动的机会(当地俱乐部、活动中心及社团等)

Purchasing your own equipment
购买自己的设备

Basic racing
基础竞赛

> Chief Instructor's/Principal's Signature
总教练/校长签字

> RYA Training Centre
RYA 培训中心

*Not necessarily applicable to keelboats. 不适用于龙骨船

ING TEAM

Level 3 – Better Sailing
级别三 进阶航海

On completion of the course the successful sailor will be safety conscious and capable of sailing without an instructor on board in light to moderate conditions. This improver course seeks to bridge the gap between Start Sailing, Basic Skills and the five Advanced modules by offering an introduction to the different modules, allowing sailors to select better their preferred route within the sport. Better Sailing is intended to make the transition easier for those sailors wishing to progress further through the scheme, allowing for opportunity to practise and consolidate sailing techniques and experience some of the activities the Advanced modules have to offer, helping to build confidence and support development of good technique and independent sailing. Additional module options are non-compulsory for completion of the Better Sailing course. They are designed to provide an introduction to the various aspects of sailing. Which elements are chosen should be discussed by student and instructor. Where practicable, students should be provided with the opportunity to sail different dinghies during the course, single and double-handers.

在完成这门课程之后，顺利通过的水手应该具备安全意识，并有能力在小到中等风速情况下独立航行。这门进阶课程的目的在于衔接“航海起步”“基础技能”和五个高级别单元。通过向学员提供关于这些单元的介绍，水手可以在这项运动中更好地选择他们喜欢的方向。“进阶航海”这门课程设置的目的是使那些希望继续在航海计划中升级的水手能够轻松地过渡，提供练习机会和巩固航海技术并体验高级别单元中的一些活动，帮助他们建立信心并提升技术和独立航行能力。附加单元是非必修内容。设计这些内容是为了介绍航海运动中的各个方面知识。选择哪些知识点应由学员和老师讨论决定。在可行的情况下，在课程中应为学员提供航行不同种类的船只、单人的和双人的机会。

Duration: Approximately 16 hours (either spread over a series of sessions or 2 full days).
时长：大约16个小时（可分为几节小课或两个整天课程）

> Practical 实践技能

Has a practical understanding of
在实践中掌握以下技能：

Sailing techniques and manoeuvres
航行技术与操控

Understands how to use rig and sail controls to prepare the boat according to different weather conditions and sea states
懂得根据不同的天气和海面情况准备索具和帆具 ☐

Can check a spinnaker is rigged correctly (if fitted)
能够检查球帆是否安装正确（如有配备） ☐

Core skills 核心技能

Can 能够：

Leave and return to a shore, jetty or mooring (including windward and leeward shore in light conditions)
驶离并返回岸边、码头或系泊处(包括在较轻的背风岸和迎风岸时) ☐

Recover a man overboard effectively
有效地救助落水人员 ☐

Use the sail telltales effectively
有效地使用帆上的风向标 ☐

Reef a sail when required
在需要时缩帆 ☐

Demonstrate a ‘dry capsize’
演示不落水的“翻船” ☐

Understands how to avoid inversion
了解如何避免船只倒置 ☐

Sail using efficient and skilful application of the Five Essentials
有效并且娴熟地应用航行五要素 ☐

Tack—maintaining boat speed and balance, upwind
迎风转向：迎风航行时保持航行速度和平衡 ☐

Gybe—maintaining boat speed and balance
顺风转向——保持航行速度和平衡

Show good use of crew and to best effect (where applicable)
良好地使用缭手达到最佳效果（当适用时）

Understands when, and the importance of manoeuvre timing 懂得何时实施操作和操作时机的重要性

> Sailing Background 航海理论知识

Has theoretical understanding of
理解如下知识：

The IRPCS, and can apply them to
知道国际海上避碰规则，并能够应用于如下情况：

Other sailing vessels 其他帆船

Power-driven vessels 机动船

Following or crossing narrow channels
沿着或穿越狭窄航道航行

Action by stand-on vessel 直航船的行动

Has basic sail-control knowledge to change the sail shape and power
具备基本的用于改变帆形和受力风帆控制知识

Understands 理解：

The points of sailing 航行角度

The Five Essentials 航行五要素

Basic meteorology terminology, including the Beaufort Scale
简单的气象学术语（包括蒲福风级标准）

Can obtain a weather forecast
能够获取天气预报

Can interpret a basic synoptic chart
能够读懂一份基本的天气图

Has awareness of changing weather conditions
具有天气情况应变的意识

> Additional Module Options
附加单元选项：

Has both practical and theoretical understanding of the following
从实践和理论两个方面理解下列单元：

Seamanship skills 航海技术

Can demonstrate anchoring in various conditions
能够在多种情况下展示锚泊

Introduction to sailing in adverse conditions (centreboardless, rudderless sailing)
在恶劣条件下航行的介绍（无稳向板或无舵航行）

Race skills 竞赛技能

Has knowledge of the 'Simplified World Sailing Racing Rules of Sailing'
了解“国际帆联简要版帆船竞赛规则”

Can 能够：

Start and finish a simple race
参加并完成一场简单的比赛

Choose the best route to sail around a course, depending on conditions (using the Five Essentials)
根据不同情况选择最佳航线（利用航行五要素）

Day sailing skills 日间航行技能

Basic chart orientation—including cardinal and lateral buoyage systems
基本的海图导航：包括方位航标和侧面航标系统

Take bearings and measure distances on a chart
在海图上测定方位及测量距离

The effect of tide and wind direction on sailing conditions
潮汐和风向对航行条件的影响

Level 3 – Better Sailing
级别三 进阶航海

Can 能够：

Use a local tide table 使用一个潮汐表

Follow a pre-planned route 按照预先计划的航线航行

Spinnaker sailing skills 球帆航行技能

Basic introduction to spinnaker handling as crew or helm, including rig, hoist and drop
掌握作为舵手或缭手操控球帆的基础知识，包括装帆、升帆和降帆

Performance sailing skills 高阶航行技能

Basic introduction to trapezing with instructor on the helm (Optional—boat—dependant)
在教练作为舵手时悬挂压舷的基础知识（可选，根据船型)

Introduction to better hiking technique 升级压舷技术的介绍

Other aspects 其他事项

The Advanced modules 高级单元

Opportunities to sail regularly 定期航行的机会

Introduction to high-performance boats 高性能船只的介绍

Local club racing 当地的俱乐部比赛

> Chief Instructor's/Principal's Signature
总教练/校长签字

> RYA Training Centre
RYA 培训中心

SEAMANSHIP SKILLS 航海技术

On successful completion of this course, you will be capable of manoeuvring a dinghy/keelboat/multihull in a seamanlike manner and making seamanship decisions in moderate conditions.

It will be assumed that when starting on this course you have already mastered the practical skills and absorbed the background knowledge required for the previous levels.

Tuition will be given by trained instructors, using appropriate supervision ratios with regard to the location and competence of the students. Much of the work afloat will be done without an instructor aboard. The emphasis is on increasing the self-reliance and decision-making of the sailor.

在成功完成这门课程后，你将能够像一名娴熟水手一样操控单人小帆船、龙骨船或多体船，并能够在中等航行条件下做出正确的决定。

我们假定你在开始学习这门课程之前，已经掌握了前面几章要求的实践技术并具备了航海理论知识。

教学由训练有素的教练员教授，使用适合教学地点和学员能力的监督比例。在水上的训练大多数由学员独立完成。这门课程的重点是提高水手的独立能力和决策能力。

Duration: Approximately 16 hours (either spread over a series of sessions or 2 full days).
时长：大约16个小时（可以分成几节小课或两个整天课程）

Practical 实操技术

Ropework 结绳术

Can tie a fisherman's bend, rolling hitch and sheet bend
能够系渔人结、轮结和单编结

Launching and recovery 下水及回岸

Can leave and return to beach, jetty or mooring, including windward and leeward shore

能够驶离并返回沙滩、码头或系泊处，包括在背风岸和迎风岸时

Sailing techniques and manoeuvres 航行技术与操控

Can 能够：

Heave to 反受风停船

Reef afloat 在水上缩帆

Recover man overboard 救助落水人员

Be towed by a power vessel
被动力艇拖拽

Anchor, including principles and techniques for different circumstances†
锚泊（包括在不同境况下的原理和技术）

Sail backwards 倒退航行

Sail in adverse circumstances (no rudder, no centreboard)*†
在恶劣条件下航行(无舵、无稳向板）*†

Knows how to prepare road trailer and secure a boat for transportation (optional)
知道如何准备路上拖车以及安全地运输船只（可选项）

Sailing Background 航海理论知识

Sailing theory and background 航行理论及背景

Understands the following terminology
理解如下术语：

Windward, leeward, abeam, forward, aft, ahead, astern, to weather, downwind, amidships, quarter, pinching, sailing by the lee, luff, bear away, planing, sternway, broaching

上风侧、下风侧、横向、船前部、船尾部、向前、向后、迎风、顺风、船中央部位、船四分之一部位、侧移、下风航行、迎风偏转、驶离风、高速滑行、船后退、船尾翘起

Knows and can apply the following International Regulations for the Prevention of Collisions at Sea (IRPCS)

知道"国际海上避碰规则"（IRPCS），并能够运用

Meeting other sailing vessels, meeting power-driven vessels, following or crossing narrow channels, action by stand-on vessel
与其他帆船相遇、与动力艇相遇或穿越狭窄通道，直航船的行动

Capsize Recovery 翻覆回正

Knows how to recover from total inversion (practical session if possible)
知道如何回正完全倒置的船只（如果可能，进行实际操作）

Meteorology 气象学

Knows sources of information on weather patterns for the day

知道当天天气变化信息的来源

Can interpret forecasts and understand local effects

能够解读天气预报并了解对当地的影响

Aware of Beaufort Wind Scale and changing weather conditions, including fog
知道蒲福风级和天气情况的变化（包括雾）

Can use local tide tables
能够运用当地的潮汐表

Understands rate of rise and fall—Twelfths Rule
了解涨潮与落潮的比率：十二分之一潮汐规则

Is aware of tidal streams 知道潮汐流

Has a basic understanding of charts and important symbols
对海图和重要的符号有基本的了解

Experienced Sailor's Direct Assesment 有经验水手的直接考核

The candidate should be able to demonstrate satisfactorily aspects of practical and theory knowledge, afloat and ashore, answering any questions.
考生应能够很好地展示航海技能和理论知识，并能够很准确地回答水上和岸上的任何问题。

Chief Instructor's/Principal's Signature
总教练/校长签字

RYA Training Centre
RYA 培训中心

*Not necessarily applicable to keelboats. 不适用于龙骨船
†Not necessarily applicable to multihulls. 不适用于多体船

DAY SAILING 日间航行

On successful completion of this course, you will have a confident, safe approach to planning and executing a short day sail in a dinghy/keelboat/multihull.

On starting this course you should have already mastered the practical skills and absorbed the background knowledge required for the previous levels. In addition, sailors wishing to cruise independently should ensure that they understand and can carry out the manoeuvres in the Seamanship Skills (see page 20) part of the RYA National Sailing Scheme.

Tuition will be given by trained instructors, supervised by a Coastal Senior Instructor, using appropriate supervision ratios with regard to the location and competence of the students. The course will include the planning and execution of a day sail.

Students will be kept informed of their individual progress throughout the course.

Candidates who hold the RYA Essential Navigation & Seamanship course completion certificate or a higher-level RYA cruising award may gain exemption from the chartwork part of Section B.

在成功完成这门课程后，你将拥有驾驶小帆船、龙骨船、多体船安全的方法进行规划和实施短途的日间航行的能力。在开始上这门课程时，你应该已经掌握了前面课程中要求的实践操作技术并学习了相关理论知识。此外，希望能够独立航行的水手应该确保自己已经理解并能够完成“航海技术”课程（参阅第20页)中的技术动作。

将由经验丰富的教练执行教学，并由另一名沿海高级教练监督，使用适合于教学地点及学员能力的监督比例。这门课程将包含日间航行的规划与执行。

在课程学习期间，学员将会被持续跟进他们的个人进展程度。

考生持有RYA航海技术基础课程结业证书或更高级别RYA巡航证书的可以免于学习B部分的海图部分。

> Duration: Approximately 16 hours (either spread over a series of sessions or 2 full days).

时长：大约16个小时（可以分为几节小课或两个整天课程）

Practical 实操技术

Rigging 装船

Can prepare and equip a boat for cruising including safety and navigation equipment, clothing and food, and stow gear correctly

能够为巡航准备及装备船只，其中包括安全及导航设备、衣服和食物以及正确的存放装备

Sailing techniques and manoeuvres 航行技术与操作

Can plan and undertake a day sail including a consideration of pilotage/navigation and collision avoidance

能够计划并进行日间航行，其中包括筹划引航/导航和避免碰撞

Can use anchor to effect lee shore landing and departure*†

能够使用锚在迎风岸时有效地登岸和离岸*†

Adverse conditions 不利条件

Is able to self-rescue following total inversion*

在船只完全倒置后能够自救*

Understands how to improvise in the event of gear failure

知道如何应对设备出现故障的情况

> Sailing Background 航海理论知识

Sailing theory and background 航海理论及背景知识

Has knowledge of boat handling in strong winds and difficult conditions (practical where possible)

熟悉在强风和恶劣条件下的船只操控（如可行时应实践）

Navigation 导航

Can plan a day's cruise in coastal waters, including knowledge of
可以在沿海水域计划一天的巡航，其中包括如下知识：

Publications available, particularly charts, tide tables, tidal stream atlases
可使用的出版物，特别是海图、潮汐表、潮汐流地图册

Navigational instruments and their limitations afloat
导航器材和它们在水上的局限

Use of GPS including waypoint navigation
全球定位系统的应用，其中包括航路点导航

Confirming position by another source
使用另一种方法确认位置

Tidal heights and tidal streams (Rule of Twelfths or percentage rule), probable changes in the weather and the interaction of weather and tidal streams
潮汐高度和潮汐流（十二分之一潮汐规则），可能出现的天气变化以及天气与潮汐流的相互作用

Decision-making in adverse circumstances including planning alternatives and refuges
在不利条件下做决定，其中包括计划备用航路和避难

Magnetic compass: Variation and Deviation
磁罗盘：变化与偏差

Interpretation of charts 解读海图

Use of transits and bearings to steer course and fix position
使用岸上参照物和方向角操纵航道并确定位置

Recording position and principles of dead reckoning
记录位置及掌握航位推测的原理

Meteorology 气象学

Knows sources of information on weather patterns for the day. Understands main characteristics of high- and low-pressure systems and simple interpretation of synoptic charts
知道当天天气情况的信息来源。了解高低压系统的主要特点和天气图的简单解读

Has awareness of changing weather conditions
具备天气条件变化的意识

> Experienced Sailor's Direct Assessment 有经验水手的直接考核

The candidate should be able to demonstrate satisfactorily competence in areas of both practical and background knowledge, ashore and afloat.

考生应能够完美地展示水上和岸上的实践能力和相关知识。

> Chief Instructor's/Principal's Signature
总教练/校长签字

> RYA Training Centre
RYA 培训中心

*Not necessarily applicable to keelboats. 不适用于龙骨船
†Not necessarily applicable to multihulls. 不适用于多体船

SAILING WITH SPINNAKERS 球帆航行技能

On successful completion of this course you will understand how to sail a dinghy/keelboat/multihull rigged with an asymmetric or symmetric spinnaker. It is assumed when starting this course you have already mastered the practical skills and absorbed the background knowledge required for previous levels. Tuition will be given by an Advanced Instructor, or by an Instructor with appropriate experience approved by the Principal, using appropriate supervision ratios with regard to the location and competence of the students.
在学完这门课程之后，你将知道如何驾驶带有对称或不对称球帆的小帆船、龙骨船或多体船。我们假定在开始学习这门课程时你已经掌握了前面课程的实践操作技术并学习了理论知识。由高级教练执教本课程，或由总负责人批准的拥有适当经验的教练执教，其将采用适合于场地及学员能力的监督比例执教。

Duration: Approximately 16 hours (either spread over a series of sessions or 2 full days).
时长：大约16个小时（可分为几节小课或两个整天课程）

Practical 实操技术

Rigging 装船

Can rig boats including spinnaker, and trapeze where fitted
能够装备船只，其中包括配有球帆和悬挂吊具时

Launching and recovery 下水和返航

Understands how to launch boats with open transoms and/or racks*†
了解如何使无艉板或带支架的船只下水*†

Sailing techniques and manoeuvres 航行技能与操控

Can sail as crew or helm using equipment to good advantage
能够作为缭手或舵手有效地使用设备

Can perform spinnaker hoist, gybe and drop as crew or helm
作为缭手或舵手都能完成球帆升帆、转向和降帆

Understands and can sail best course downwind
理解并能以最佳航线顺风航行

Capsize recovery 翻覆回正

Can perform capsize recovery including spinnaker
可以完成带有球帆的翻覆回正

Knows how to recover from total inversion*
知道如何回正一只完全倒置的船只*

Sailing Background 航海理论知识

Racing 竞赛

Has knowledge of courses for type of boat
了解不同船型的特定航线

Sailing theory and background 航海理论及背景知识

Understands the concept of apparent wind sailing
了解航行风的概念

Understands the effect of hull shape on performance
了解船体形状对航行的影响

Can access sources of information and apply rig set-up for different conditions
能够根据不同条件进行船只配置并能够获取相关信息

Experienced Sailor's Direct Assessment 有经验水手的直接考核

Candidates should be able to demonstrate competence and confidence in areas afloat and ashore, practical and of sailing background.
考生因能够完美地展示水上和岸上的技能和相关知识。

Chief Instructor's/Principal's Signature
总教练/校长签字

RYA Training Centre
RYA 培训中心

*Not necessarily applicable to keelboats. 不适用于龙骨船
†Not necessarily applicable to multihulls. 不适用于多体船

RS
Feva

PERFORMANCE SAILING
高阶航海

On successful completion of this course, you will understand how to sail performance dinghies/keelboats/multihulls in all wind conditions that you can expect to encounter, sailing the boat to best advantage at all times. The emphasis is on coaching to improve your sailing performance and therefore will involve coaching from powerboats. This course is intended primarily for two–person spinnaker boats; however, it may be delivered in performance single–handers and the certificate endorsed accordingly.

Tuition will be given by an Advanced Instructor for the type of boat, using appropriate supervision ratios with regard to the location and competence of the students and the need to provide continuous feedback on the water. It is assumed that every student starting this course has already mastered the practical skills and absorbed the background knowledge required for previous levels. In practical terms, at least a full season' s sailing experience since learning to sail is advisable.

在学习完这门课程之后，你将了解如何在所有可能遇到的风况下驾驶高性能小帆船、龙骨船和多体船，并在任何时候操纵船只达到最佳航行效果。本部分内容重点在于指导你们提升航海水平，因此部分教学是在动力艇上进行的。这门课程主要针对双人带球帆船只；然而，在单人高性能船只上也可能教授该内容，并颁发相应证书。

教学由负责相应船只的高级教练教授，其会根据教学场地及学员能力以及要在水上提供教学的需要采用相应的监督比例。我们希望每名学员在开始学习这门课程之前已经掌握了前面级别的实践技能并学习了相关理论知识。具体而言，我们建议学员至少拥有一整个航海季的航海经验。

Duration: Approximately 16 hours (either spread over a series of sessions or 2 full days).
课时：大约16小时（可分为几节小课或两个整天课程）

› Practical 实操技术

Rigging 装船

Can rig any type of boat, including spinnaker and trapeze (if fitted)
能够装备任何种类的船只，其中包括球帆和悬挂吊索（如有安装）

Understands basic rig setup and tuning
了解基本的装船步骤与调校

Sailing techniques and manoeuvres 航行技术与操控

Can make best possible use of crew and equipment to sail efficiently on all points of sailing in a variety of conditions, including symmetric or asymmetric spinnaker
能够较好地使用缭手和设备在不同航行条件下沿任意航行角度有效地航行，其中包括在配有对称或不对称球帆时

Can use sail controls to effect changes to shape and power of sails
能够使用船帆控制索有效地调节船帆形状及受力

Can spot and use windshifts and gusts to effect best course up and down wind
在迎风和顺风时都能够发现和利用风摆及阵风调节最佳航道

Can perform capsize recovery including spinnaker. Knows how to recover from total inversion*
可以完成翻覆回正，其中包括带有球帆时。知道如何从完全倒置中回正*

Can tack, refining skills according to conditions
能够迎风转向，并能够根据不同条件精确地应用操作技术

Shows understanding of roll tacking principles
理解滚动迎风转向的原则

Can gybe, refining skills according to conditions
能够顺风转向，并能够根据不同条件精确地应用操作技术

Shows understanding of roll gybing principles 理解滚动顺风转向的原则

Sailing Background
航海理论知识

Sailing theory and background
航行理论及背景

Understands how to make use of wind variation and tidal eddies which occur due to geographical features and tidal conditions
了解如何利用由于地形地貌和潮汐情况而产生的不同风况以及潮汐漩涡

Has an understanding of hull shapes and rig types, including their effect on performance 了解不同的船体形状和船桅种类，其中包括它们对于航行的影响

Understands planing and the effect of rails
了解高速滑行和船侧水流对航向的影响

Meteorology 气象学

Knows sources of information on weather patterns for the day
知道当天天气信息情况

Understands main characteristics of high– and low–pressure systems and simple interpretation of synoptic charts
了解高压和低压系统的主要特征以及气象图的简单解读

Has awareness of changing weather conditions 有应对天气情况变化的意识

Experienced Sailor's Direct Assessment
有经验水手的直接考核

Candidates should show confidence and competence in practical and sailing background areas, both afloat and ashore.
考生应能够展示其在水上和岸上航海技能方面的自信和相关技能水平。

Chief Instructor's/Principal's Signature
总教练/校长签字

RYA Training Centre
RYA 培训中心

*Not necessarily applicable to keelboats. 不适用于龙骨船

RYA SAILFOILING COURSES:FIRST FLIGHTS
RYA 水翼船课程：第一次航行

This first session in SAILfoiling provides an initial introduction into the amazing and exhilarating world of foiling. As a pre-requisite, you should hold the RYA Level 2 Basic Skills, which will ensure you have the necessary skills to take on foiling! Aimed as a taster session, First Flights provides you with a basic introduction to foiling, assisting you to make your first foiling take-offs. Suggested course length: Two to four hours (taster session).

在学习完这门课程之后，你将了解如何在所有可能遇到的风况下驾驶高性能小帆船、龙骨水翼航行的第一次培训，将会提供一个令人惊叹与兴奋的水翼世界的初步介绍。作为前提条件，你应该持有RYA二级证书并掌握基础技能，这将确保你已经掌握必要的技能能够驾驶水翼船！作为体验课程，第一次航行为你提供了水翼航行的基本知识介绍，这将助力你的第一次水翼起航。建议课程时长：2～4小时（体验课程）。

Practical实操技术

Rigging装船

Has knowledge of 了解

Assembling and setting up the main foil, rudder, and rudder foil
组装和调试主翼、舵和舵翼

Various foiling boats
各种水翼船

The options and adaptions available for non-foiling boats.
非翼船的选择和改装

Launching and Recovery 下水和回岸

Has knowledge of the different launch/recovery methods for different boat designs.
对于不同的船型设计，了解其不同的下水和回岸的方法。

Sailing Techniques and Manoeuvres 航行技术和操纵

Can能够

Engage and disengage foils
拆装翼

Change course sailed, and adjust sail trim to encourage flight.
改变航向，并调整风帆配平以利航行。

Take off.
改变航向，并调整风帆配平已利航行。

Understands and has knowledge of: 理解并了解：

How to land safely.
如何安全着陆。

How to maintain foiling.
如何保持水翼航行。

Capsize recovery methods.
翻覆时的回正方法。

Apparent wind, showing a basic application and sail adjustment.
视风，展示基本应用和航行调整。

FOILING KNOWLEDGE水翼船基本知识

Understands and has knowledge of 理解并了解：

The basic theory of how foils work.
水翼工作原理的基本理论。

A range of different foiling boats.
一系列不同的船。

Sail adjustments, and how to trim sails.
帆的调整，以及如何调帆。

SAFETY 安全

Understands and has knowledge of 理解并了解：

The risks of foiling alone.
水翼船独自航行的风险。

The lack of noise when approaching other craft.
接近其他船只时无噪音。

Different personal safety equipment.
不同的个人安全设备。

The importance of foiling in suitable sailing conditions.
在适当的航行条件下进行水翼航行的重要性。

Chief Instructor's/Principal's Signature
总教练/校长签字

RYA Training Centre
RYA 培训中心

Photo credit:Paul Wyeth

SUSTAINED FLIGHTS 持续航行

Sustained Flights is designed to increase your foil handling and control. Having completed this course, you will start to feel more confident about the practical techniques and theory required to foil, steer, and maintain a course effectively. All tacking or gybing at this level is non–foiling.

It will be assumed that every student starting this course has already mastered the practical skills and absorbed the background knowledge required for First Flights. Suggested course length: Up to 16 hours, either spread over a series of sessions or full days.

持续航行的目的是增加你对翼处理和控制的能力。完成本课程后，你将开始对实操技术和水翼所需的理论、角度调整、有效地保持航线有更多的自信。在这个水平上的所有固缝或回转都是非水翼的。

假设每一个开始学习这门课程的学员都已经掌握了相应技能，并且掌握了第一次航行所需的相关知识。建议课程长度：长达16小时，可分为一系列课程或全天。

> Practical 实操技术

RIGGING 索具

Can assemble and set up the main foil (with assistance)
可以组装和设置主翼（需要帮助） ☐

Can assemble and set up the rudder and rudder foil (with assistance)
可以装配和设置舵和舵翼（需要帮助） ☐

Has knowledge of how to adjust foils in different conditions to optimise performance
了解在不同条件下如何调整翼以优化性能 ☐

Understands how to trim the main foil to adjust the 'ride height'
了解如何修正主翼以便调整"航行高度" ☐

> LAUNCHING AND RECOVERY 下水和回岸

Can 能够

Launch the boat off a slipway/beach using a method specific for that foiling boat (with assistance)
使用水翼船特定的方法在坡道/沙滩下水(在有辅助的情况下) ☐

Safely return to slipway/beach using a method specific to that foiling boat
使用水翼船特定的操船方法安全返回坡道/海滩 ☐

> SAILING TECHNIQUE AND MANOEUVRES 航行技术与操纵

Can 能够

Maintain periods of sustained foiling
保持持续的水翼航行 ☐

Trim sails effectively according to the apparent wind
根据视风有效地调整帆 ☐

Photo credit:Paul Wyeth

Demonstrate a non-foiling tack
演示非水翼船的迎风转向

Demonstrate a non-foiling gybe
演示非水翼船的顺风转向

Adjust bow height and trim through the rudder foil
调整船头高度并通过舵翼进行调节

Show basic skills and understanding of foiling on various points of sail
演示基本技能和理解各个不同的水翼航行角度

FOILING KNOWLEDGE 水翼船知识

Technique 技术：

Understands the apparent-wind effect and how to trim effectively according to the point of sail
了解视风效应及如何根据航行角度进行有效调帆

Understands different ride heights and how to adjust the main foil to enable the boat to ride higher or lower
了解不同的航行高度以及如何调整主翼片，使船能够航行得更高或更低

Has knowledge of correct angles for tack entry and exit
了解迎风转向前后的正确角度

Has knowledge of correct angles for gybe entry and exit
了解顺风转向前后的正确角度

Theory 理论

Understands 了解：

How the wand works
尾翼调整杆的工作原理

How twist tillers adjust the rudder
如何扭转舵柄调整方向舵

Righting moment and how it is achieved
矫正时机及其实现方法

SAFETY 安全

Has knowledge of safety equipment which may be worn while foiling
了解在水翼航行时可能需要佩戴的安全护具

Chief Instructor's/Principal's Signature
总教练/校长签字

RYA Training Centre
RYA 培训中心

Photo credit:Paul Wyeth

PERFORMANCE FLIGHTS
高性能航行

Performance Flights is the last of the RYA foiling courses, looking at advanced skills and technique. This course will increase your confidence on different angles, while also looking at entry and exit into manoeuvres, providing you with a good understanding as to the theory.

It will be assumed that every student starting this course has the knowledge and practical ability of RYA Sustained Flights or above.

Suggested course length: Up to 16 hours, either spread over a series of sessions or full days.

高性能航行是RYA最后的水翼船课程，课程注重卓越的技能和技术。这门课程将增加你在多种情况下的信心，同时也会为您提供观看起航和结束航行演练过程的机会，以增强理论理解。

我们假定每一个开始学习这门课程的学员都具备RYA持续航行或以上的知识和实践的能力。

建议课程长度：最长16小时，可以在一系列课程中进行，也可以在一整天中进行。

Practical 实操技术

SAILING TECHNIQUE AND MANOEUVRES 航行技术和操纵

Can 能够：

Demonstrate foiling upwind and downwind
演示迎风和顺风的水翼航行

Effectively set up, balance, and steer into the tack
有效地设置、平衡和转向

Demonstrate tack entry while foiling, exiting in control
演练水翼航行时迎风转向开始方法，在可控下结束

Can 能够

Effectively set up, balance, and steer into the gybe
顺风转向时有效地设置、平衡和回转

Demonstrate gybe entry while foiling, exiting in control
演示顺风转向的水翼航行进入、退出控制

FOILING KNOWLEDGE 水翼航行知识

Can 能够

Steer and adopt the correct body movements required to foil through a gybe
引导并采用正确的身体动作，以完成顺风转向

Adjust wand settings and ride height for optimum performance in different conditions
调整控制尾翼调整杆设置和底盘高度，以在不同条件下获得最佳性能

Understands 了解：

The theory and technique required to set up and approach the 'entry' of a foiling tack and gybe
水翼迎风转向和顺风转向的准备和开始（航行）方法所需的理论和技术

The theory and technique required to set up and approach the 'exit' for a foiling tack and gybe
水翼迎风转向和顺风转向的准备和结束方法所需的理论和技术

What causes and how to deal with a pitch pole (specific boats)
什么原因以及如何处理纵摇杆（特定船只）

Different wand systems and what they are used for
不同的尾翼调整杆系统及其用途

SAFETY 安全

Understands the importance of safe sailing areas and suitable sailing conditions to assist with the practise of performance foiling manoeuvres
了解安全航行区域和适当航行条件的重要性，以帮助练习高性能水翼航行时的动作

Chief Instructor's/Principal's Signature
总教练/校长签字

RYA Training Centre
RYA 培训中心

Photo credit Paul Wyeth

START RACING 初级竞赛

This course is designed to give the confidence, skills and knowledge to take part in club racing in good conditions. Confidence is essential if the sailor is to enjoy racing. The course involves the sailor in a range of enjoyable exercises designed to build confidence and to improve skills through practice. It is assumed that every student starting this course has already mastered the practical skills and absorbed the background knowledge required for previous levels.
这门课程的目的是给予学员信心、技能和知识，从而以良好的状态参加俱乐部的竞赛。水手如果希望参加竞赛，信心是必不可少的。这门课程使水手参与一系列愉快的练习，建立其信心并通过实践增强其技能。我们希望每位学员在开始学习这门课程时已经掌握了前面课程的实践技能并学习了所需的理论知识。

Physical and mental preparation 体力与心理的准备

Has knowledge of 了解如下知识：

- Food as fuel 补充能量的食物
- Keeping hydrated 注意饮水，保持身体水分

Boat preparation 船只准备

Has knowledge of 了解如下知识：

- Availability of class tuning guides 拥有级别的船只调校指南
- Basic tuning 基本的调校知识

Boat handling 控船

Has a basic understanding of 简单地了解如下知识：

- Making best use of the Five Essentials as Helm 作为舵手熟练地使用航行五要素
- Crew (Double-handers only) 缭手（只适用于双人船）
- Mark rounding 绕标
- Laylines 方位线
- Hiking 压舷

Boat speed 船速

- Understands how to alter sail controls both round the course and for differing conditions 了解在整条航线的不同位置或应对不同条件如何调节帆的控制索

Teamwork (for double-handers) 团队协作（双人船）

- Understands the requirements to develop a good partnership 懂得如何搞好伙伴关系

Strategy and meteorology 策略和气象学

- Can obtain and understand a simple weather forecast 能够获取并解读一份简单的天气预报
- Has knowledge of clean air, gusts and lulls 了解干净风、阵风和间歇风的知识

Racing rules 竞赛规则

- Has a basic understanding of the Racing Rules of Sailing (part 2, section a) 对帆船的竞赛规则有基本的了解（第2部分，第一节）

Has an understanding of the basic rights of way rules 对基础的航行权规则有所了解：

- Port/starboard (rule 10) 左舷船让右舷船（第十条规则）
- Windward boat (rule 11) 上风船让下风船（第十一条规则）
- Clear ahead/clear astern (rule 12) 后船让前船(第十二条规则)
- Tacking (rule 13) 迎风转向（第十三条规则）

Tactics 策略

Has knowledge of basic boat-on-boat situations
了解处理船与船的基本关系

Starts 起航

Has knowledge of transits 懂得参照线

Can demonstrate the basics of starting
能够展示起航的基本技巧

Other aspects 其他事项

An introduction to local club racing
当地俱乐部竞赛的介绍

> Chief Instructor's/Principal's Signature
总教练/校长签字

> RYA Training Centre
RYA 培训中心

INTERMEDIATE RACING 中级竞赛

This course builds on the knowledge and skills learnt from ‘Start Racing’, developing greater awareness of the key principles of starting, boat handling, boat speed, strategy and tactics, through course time and regular race activity.
这门课程建立在“初级竞赛”技能的基础之上，通过绕标练习和日常比赛深化起航、控船、船速、战略战术的基本原则的认识。

Physical and mental preparation 体力和心理的准备

Understands the importance of fitness for sailing
了解健身对航行的重要性 □

Boat preparation 船只准备

Has knowledge of 了解如下知识：

How to use a tuning guide
如何使用调校指南 □

How to set a boat up for specific conditions
如何为特定条件设置船只 □

Understands 了解：

How to prepare a boat for club racing, including
如何为俱乐部竞赛准备船只，包括：

- Hull 船体 □
- Spars 船桅部件 □
- Sails 帆 □
- Foils 片状部件 □
- Fittings 固定装置 □
- Rigging 装船 □
- Control lines 控制绳 □

Boat handling 船只操控

Has knowledge of how to steer the boat without the rudder
懂得无舵航行 □

Understands the principles involved in
理解如下原则：

Slow-speed handling, including
低速航行操控，包括：

- Stopping 停船 □
- Accelerating 加速 □
- Sailing backwards 倒退航行 □
- Roll tacking 滚动迎风转向 □
- Roll gybing 滚动顺风转向 □

Boat speed 船速

Has knowledge of basic aerodynamics
具备基本的空气动力学知识：

- How a sail works 帆如何工作 □
- How to power up the rig 如何给帆加力 □
- How to de-power the rig 如何给帆减力 □
- Weather helm 上风舵 □
- Lee helm 下风舵 □

Understands how to set up the boat for a range of conditions
了解如何为一系列条件装配船 □

Teamwork (double-handers) 团队协作（双人航行）

Understands how to divide up the
了解如何做如下的分工：

Roles around the course
在航线上各个位置的角色 □

Jobs in the boat 船上的工作 □

Strategy and meteorology 竞赛策略和气象学

Understands 了解：

- Clean air 干净风 □
- Gusts 阵风 □
- Lulls 间歇风 □

How to interpret a weather forecast in relation to the sailing venue
如何解读相关场地的天气预报 □

Racing rules 竞赛规则

Understands 理解：

Has a good understanding of Part 1/Section A and the Definitions of the Racing Rules
对第一部分/A部分以及竞赛规则定义有很好的理解 □

Basic understanding of Sections B/C/D
对B部分、C部分和D部分有基本的理解 □

Understands how to sail by the Racing Rules

了解如何根据竞赛规则航行

Tactics 竞赛战术

Understands 理解：

Boat-on-boat tactics 船挨船的战术

Lee bow situation 下风船的战术

How to cover and break cover
如何遮挡及摆脱遮挡

Importance of clean air 干净风的重要性

Starts 起航

Understands bias, and how to assess it
了解起航线偏转原因并知道如何应对

Has knowledge of 了解如下知识：

How to hold boat on line (hovering)
如何保持船只在起航线上（迎风停船）

Accelerating off the line 起航后加速

Other aspects 其他事项

Has knowledge of and participates regularly in club and open meetings
知道竞赛信息的来源以及定期参与俱乐部竞赛和公开赛

> Chief Instructor's/Principal's Signature
总教练/校长签字

> RYA Training Centre
RYA 培训中心

ADVANCED RACING 高级竞赛

A predominately practical course, Advanced Racing is all about developing skills in preparation for open meetings and higher-level competition.
“高级竞赛”课程以实践操作为主，其可以提高你参加公开赛或更高级别的竞赛的技能水平。

Mental and physical preparation 体力和心理的准备

Understands how to, and the value of, goal setting
了解如何制定目标及其意义

Boat preparation 船只准备

Understands how to 了解如何：

- Improve foil finish 打磨片状部件
- Optimise boat to class rules 调控船只符合级别的规定
- Use a tuning guide 使用调校指南

Boat handling 船只操控

Understands the principles of 了解如下原则：

- Steering with sails 使用帆控制方向
- Balance 平衡

Can demonstrate these principles in taking penalty turns
在执行犯规转圈时能展示这些原则

Can demonstrate good techniques in a full range of conditions
能在各种条件下良好地展示航行技能：

- Tacking 迎风转向
- Gybing 顺风转向

Boat speed 船速

Understands 理解：

- Relevance of sail controls and effects on the sail(s)
  帆的控制索及其对帆的作用
- How to change gears in different conditions while on the water
  在水上时，如何根据不同条件调节装备
- How to vary the tuning guide for different conditions
  如何针对不同的航行条件修改调校指南
- How to create your own tuning guide
  如何创建自己的调校指南
- How to create your own post-race analysis sheet
  如何创建自己的赛后分析表

Teamwork (double-handers) 团队协作（双人船）

Understands effective 有效地理解：

- Race analysis 竞赛分析
- Race and training goals 赛前训练目标

Can 能够：

- Communicate effectively 高效地交流
- React to changing circumstances
  应对环境的变化

Strategy and meteorology 策略及气象学

Can create a race strategy prior to going afloat based on weather forecasts and tide tables etc
能够在航行前根据天气预报和潮汐表等信息制订比赛策略

Racing rules 竞赛规则

Has good knowledge and understanding of the Racing Rules of Sailing, Part 2
对帆船竞赛规则有良好地认识和理解，第2部分

Understands the RYA Racing Charter
了解RYA竞赛章程

Tactics 竞赛战术

Has knowledge of 掌握如下知识：

- Holding a lane upwind 保持上风航线
- Boat-on-fleet tactics 船队战术
- Attacking 进攻
- Controlling situations 控制情况

Understands 了解：

- Boat-on-group tactics 小组战术
- Overtaking and defending tactics
  超越和防守战术
- Covering 遮挡
- Different approaches to marks—when to gybe or bear away
  靠近浮标的不同方法，何时顺风转向以及驶向下风

Starts 起航

Understands pre-start rules
了解预备起航规则

Can 能够：

Protect a gap to leeward
在下风处留出空间

Hold the boat on the line (hovering)
保持船只在起航线上（迎风停船）

Use transits 使用参照线

Has knowledge of 了解如下知识：

Various start sequences 不同的起航序列

Recall signals 召回信号

Starting penalties 抢航处罚

Other aspects 其他事项

Participates regularly in 定期参与：

Open meetings 公开赛

National class events 国家级别赛事

> Chief Instructor's/Principal's Signature
总教练/校长签字

> RYA Training Centre
RYA 培训中心

INSTRUCTOR TRAINING 教练员培训

If you have enjoyed your experiences of learning to sail and developing your sailing techniques and skills through the RYA National Sailing Scheme, why not consider sharing your enthusiasm, expertise and skills with others by becoming involved in the RYA instructor training programme? Below are brief details concerning the basic training courses. More information can be found in G14 RYA National Sailing Scheme Instructor Handbook.

RYA Assistant Instructor

Duration: 2 days / 20 hours

The RYA Assistant Instructor is trained to assist qualified instructors to teach beginners up to the standard of the RYA National Sailing Scheme Level 2 and the RYA Youth Sailing Scheme Stage 3. They must only work under the supervision of a Senior Instructor. The award is centre–specific.

Eligibility for the training course

Pass one of the RYA National Sailing Scheme Advanced Modules or equivalent personal sailing standard.

Recommendation by Principal of training centre.

Training

Training will cover the centre's safe–operation procedures and the teaching points related to teaching beginners. The award is centre–specific. Training is based on a two–day or modular course of 20 hours' duration at the centre run by the Principal/Chief Instructor who holds a valid RYA Senior Instructor certificate.

Assessment

Candidates will be assessed on their practical teaching ability with beginners. Successful candidates will be awarded an RYA Assistant Instructor certificate by their Principal.

教练员培训 INSTRUCTOR TRAINING

如果你喜欢通过RYA国家航海计划学习航海并提高你的航海技能和技巧，那么为什么不考虑通过参加RYA教练员培训计划把你的激情、专长和技能分享给其他人呢？如下是关于基础培训课程的基本详情。更多信息可以在RYA编码为G14的《国家航海计划教练员手册》中找到。

RYA助理教练员课程

时长：两天或20个小时

RYA助理教练接受培训达到能协助正式教练指导初学者达到RYA国家航海计划第二级别以及RYA青少年航海计划的第三阶段。
他们只能在高级教练的监督下授课。裁定由机构具体政策决定。

课程培训所需资格

通过RYA国家航海计划高级别单元中的一个或者相等的个人航海水平。

必须得到培训中心总负责人的推荐。

培训内容

培训将包括培训中心的安全操作章程以及与培训初学者有关的教学要点。
证书将由培训中心颁发。培训是基于两个整天的课程或者总时长为20个小时的多节小课并由持有RYA高级教练证书的中心总负责人/总教练主持。

考核

考核将针对考生对于初学者的实践教授能力。成功通过的学员将会由总教练授予RYA助理教练证书。

Dinghy/Keelboat/Multihull Instructor 小帆船、龙骨船、多体帆船教练员课程

Duration: 5 days / 50 hours
时长：5天或50个小时

It is possible to complete the RYA National Sailing Scheme in dinghies, keelboats or multihulls. Therefore, instructors teaching the scheme must be qualified for the type of boat in which they will be teaching. The instructor certificate will show whether the instructor is qualified to teach on inland or coastal waters (depending on where they completed the pre-entry sailing assessment and course).
RYA国家航海教学计划的全部课程在小帆船、龙骨船或者多体船上完成都是可行的。因此教练员在教授RYA航海计划时必须已取得课程要求所采用船只的教学资格。教练员证书上会标明该名教练是否被授予内湖教学或沿海教学的资格（这取决于他们在哪里完成的课前航海测试以及培训课程）。

Role 角色

- Competent, experienced sailor able to sail in strong winds
有能力和经验在强风中航行的水手
- Can teach RYA National Sailing Scheme up to and including Seamanship Skills, Day Sailing, Sailing with Spinnakers and RYA Youth Sailing Scheme Stages 1 - 4
可以教授RYA国家航海计划，其包括航海技术技能、日间航行、球帆航行技能和RYA青少年航海计划第一到第四阶段的课程
- Will only work under the supervision of the RYA Senior Instructor
必须在RYA高级教练的监督下工作

Eligibility for the training course
参与培训课程所需要的资格

- Minimum age 16 最小16周岁
- Valid first aid certificate 有效的急救证书 (see www.rya.org.uk/go/firstaidcertificates)
- RYA Powerboat Level 2 certificate RYA动力艇第二级别证书
- Pre-entry sailing assessment completed
通过课前航海测试
- RYA membership 成为RYA会员

Training 培训内容

- The structure and content of the RYA National Sailing Scheme and RYA Youth Sailing Scheme
RYA国家航海教学计划和RYA青少年航海教学计划的结构及内容
- Training in RYA teaching methods including teaching both adults and children采用RYA教学方法教学包括成人教学和青少年教学
- Preparation and presentation of a lesson
准备及演示一个课程
- Preparation and use of visual aids
准备及使用视觉辅助
- The assessment of students’ abilities
考核学员的能力
- The use of powered craft in a teaching environment 在教学环境中动力艇的使用

Assessment 考核

- The assessment will be based on an overall (or holistic) judgement throughout the week and during the instructor moderation day

考核将在一个星期的考核期内以及考核日当天进行整体的（或全面的）评估

This assessment will include
这个考核将包括:

- Enthusiasm for the sport
  对于这门运动的热情
- Sailing ability 航海能力
- Confidence and knowledge in the subject
  对于科目所拥有的信心和知识
- Awareness of safety 安全意识
- Practical teaching according to RYA methods
  按照RYA方法的实践教学
- Theory knowledge 理论知识
- Successful demonstrations and clear explanations
  成功地的展示和清晰地解释
- Correct diagnosis and tactful correction of students' faults
  正确地诊断和婉转地纠正学员错误
- Safe powerboat handling in a teaching environment
  在教学环境里安全地驾驶动力艇

PERSONAL LOG 个人日志

日期	船只类型	小时经验		活动与天气条件		批准
		舵手	撩手	航线种类或活动	最大风速	培训中心/俱乐部教练

个人日志 PERSONAL LOG

日期	船只类型	小时经验		活动与天气条件		批准
		舵手	撩手	航线种类或活动	最大风速	培训中心/俱乐部教练

PLEASE ATTACH YOUR RYA CERTIFICATE HERE

请把证书贴在这里

Please note that no record of certificates is held by the RYA

请注意RYA不为证书做记录

Enquiries about lost certificates should be made to the centre where the course was taken

询问有关证书遗失应与
该证书的颁发培训机构联系

PLEASE ATTACH YOUR
RYA CERTIFICATE HERE

请把证书贴在这里

Please note that no record of certificates is held by the RYA

请注意RYA不为证书做记录

Enquiries about lost certificates should be made to the centre where the course was taken

询问有关证书遗失应与该证书的颁发培训机构联系

COURSE CERTIFICATES 结课证书

PLEASE ATTACH YOUR
RYA CERTIFICATE HERE

请把证书贴在这里

Please note that no record of certificates is held by the RYA

请注意RYA不为证书做记录

Enquiries about lost certificates should be made to the centre where the course was taken

询问有关证书遗失应与
该证书的颁发培训机构联系

**PLEASE ATTACH YOUR
RYA CERTIFICATE HERE**

请把证书贴在这里

Please note that no record of
certificates is held by the RYA

请注意RYA不为证书做记录

Enquiries about lost certificates
should be made to the centre
where the course was taken

询问有关证书遗失应与
该证书的颁发培训机构联系

COURSE CERTIFICATES 结课证书

PLEASE ATTACH YOUR
RYA CERTIFICATE HERE

请把证书贴在这里

Please note that no record of certificates is held by the RYA

请注意RYA不为证书做记录

Enquiries about lost certificates should be made to the centre where the course was taken

询问有关证书遗失应与该证书的颁发培训机构联系

**PLEASE ATTACH YOUR
RYA CERTIFICATE HERE**

请把证书贴在这里

Please note that no record of
certificates is held by the RYA

请注意RYA不为证书做记录

Enquiries about lost certificates
should be made to the centre
where the course was taken

询问有关证书遗失应与
该证书的颁发培训机构联系

COURSE CERTIFICATES 结课证书

PLEASE ATTACH YOUR
RYA CERTIFICATE HERE

请把证书贴在这里

Please note that no record of certificates is held by the RYA

请注意RYA不为证书做记录

Enquiries about lost certificates should be made to the centre where the course was taken

询问有关证书遗失应与该证书的颁发培训机构联系

PLEASE ATTACH YOUR
RYA CERTIFICATE HERE

请把证书贴在这里

Please note that no record of certificates is held by the RYA

请注意RYA不为证书做记录

Enquiries about lost certificates should be made to the centre where the course was taken

询问有关证书遗失应与
该证书的颁发培训机构联系

PLEASE ATTACH YOUR
RYA CERTIFICATE HERE

请把证书贴在这里

Please note that no record of certificates is held by the RYA

请注意RYA不为证书做记录

Enquiries about lost certificates should be made to the centre where the course was taken

询问有关证书遗失应与
该证书的颁发培训机构联系

RYA

PLEASE ATTACH YOUR RYA CERTIFICATE HERE

请把证书贴在这里

Please note that no record of certificates is held by the RYA

请注意RYA不为证书做记录

Enquiries about lost certificates should be made to the centre where the course was taken

询问有关证书遗失应与该证书的颁发培训机构联系

黑版贸审字 08-2020-066

内容简介：

本书主要介绍了英国皇家游艇协会航海培训的国家级教学计划，以及航海起步、进阶航海、高阶航海等不同阶段和初级竞赛、中级竞赛、高级竞赛等不同级别应该掌握的技能水平要求、装备准备、技术要点等内容。

本书适合帆船爱好者及帆船培训机构使用。

图书在版编目（CIP）数据

国家航海计划教学大纲及日志 / 英国皇家游艇协会著；顾禹译. -- 哈尔滨：哈尔滨工程大学出版社，2020.4

ISBN 978-7-5661-2624-5

Ⅰ. ①国… Ⅱ. ①英… ②顾… Ⅲ. ①帆船运动－青少年读物 Ⅳ. ①G861.4-49

中国版本图书馆 CIP 数据核字（2020）第 054169 号

选题策划　史大伟　薛　力
责任编辑　唐欢欢
封面设计　李海波

出版发行　哈尔滨工程大学出版社
社　　址　哈尔滨市南岗区南通大街 145 号
邮政编码　150001
发行电话　0451-82519328
传　　真　0451-82519699
经　　销　新华书店
印　　刷　武汉精一佳印刷有限公司
开　　本　787 mm×1 092 mm　1/32
印　　张　1.875
字　　数　109 千字
版　　次　2020 年 4 月第 1 版
印　　次　2020 年 4 月第 1 次印刷
定　　价　60.00 元
http：//www.hrbeupress.com
E-mail：heupress@hrbeu.edu.cn